GRAPHIC BATTLES OF THE CIVIL WAR™

# THE BATTLE OF
# GETTYSBURG

## Spilled Blood on Sacred Ground

By **Dan Abnett** *Illustrated by* **Dheeraj Verma**

New York

Published in 2007 by The Rosen Publishing Group, Inc.
29 East 21st Street, New York, NY 10010

First edition, 2007

Photo Credits: p. 4 (top) Courtesy of Military Images Magazine, (bottom) Harper's Weekly; p. 5 Harper's Weekly; p. 7 (top) Harper's Weekly, (bottom) Courtesy of Anne S. K. Brown Military Collection, Brown University Library; p. 44 Hulton Getty, p. 45 (top) Courtesy of Anne S. K. Brown Military Collection, Brown University Library, (bottom) Library of Congress

Simone Drinkwater, Series Editor/Osprey Publishing
Nel Yomtov, Series Editor/Rosen Book Works
Geeta Sobha, Editor/Rosen Book Works

Library of Congress Cataloging-in-Publication Data

Abnett, Dan.
  The Battle of Gettysburg : spilled blood on sacred ground / by Dan Abnett. —
  1st ed.
  p. cm. — (Graphic battles of the Civil War)
  Includes bibliographical references and index.
  ISBN-13      978-1-4042-0777-6 (lib.)        978-1-4042-6477-9 (pbk.)
  ISBN-10      1-4042-0777-5  (lib.)            1-4042-6477-9    (pbk.)
  6-pack ISBN-13   978-1-4042-6272-0            6-pack ISBN-10   1-4042-6272-5
  1. Gettysburg, Battle of, Gettysburg, Pa., 1863—Juvenile literature. I. Title. II.
  Series.

E475.53.A23 200
973.7'349—dc22

                                                    2006014272

# CONTENTS

## THE AMERICAN CIVIL WAR, 1861 – 1865

The first shots of the Civil War were fired on April 12, 1861, when Southern forces bombed Fort Sumter, in South Carolina. The nation had been heading toward conflict for many years because of the economic and political differences between Northern and Southern states. The biggest difference was over slavery. In the South, slavery was legal. Slavery was illegal in the North.

Both North and South had advantages in the war. The North had more manufacturing and a better railroad system. The South, especially at the beginning of the war, had better military leaders. They also knew they only had to fight long enough for the North to give up hope of bringing the states that had seceded, or left the Union, back in.

Many famous battles were fought during the four-year struggle, but none is more famous than the Battle of Gettysburg, fought from July 1 to July 3, 1863. On those days, the course of American history was forever changed.

## KEY COMMANDERS

**MAJ. GEN. GEORGE G. MEADE**
Meade took charge of the Army of the Potomac days before Gettysburg. Earlier, he had led a successful offensive at Fredricksburg in December 1862.

**COL. JOSHUA CHAMBERLAIN**
The hero of Little Round Top, holding the high ground and the Union line at Gettysburg, he was awarded the Medal of Honor.

**LT. GEN. JAMES LONGSTREET**
Nicknamed "Old Warhorse," he was dependable, but sometimes slow to act on orders because he tended to be cautious.

**MAJ. GEN. GEORGE E. PICKETT**
Perhaps the most fear-less—yet tragic—figure at Gettysburg. The disastrous charge he led was later named after him.

In the summer of 1863, Confederate States of America (CSA) president Jefferson Davis and Confederate general Robert E. Lee developed a plan to solve several problems that Southern forces were facing in the fighting of the Civil War.

Although the Confederates had enough men in their armies at this time, uniforms, equipment, and medical supplies were often hard to come by. The lack of industry in the South was a major cause of this problem.

Food was also often in low supply. To make the situation worse, the South was trying to avoid fighting on its own land in order to protect the crops it grew for its armies.

General Lee proposed a plan for the Confederates to fight a major battle

★ Gen. George Gordon Meade

★ *Union general George Gordon Meade replaced General Hooker as commander of the Army of the Potomac in June 1863. He led the army until the end of the war.*

★ Jefferson Davis

★ *Jefferson Davis was elected the first and only president of the Confederate States of America.*

on Northern soil, so that crops in Southern states could be harvested and food supplies for the army increased. Meanwhile, the Confederates could live off the lands in the North, so that their immediate needs were met.

General Lee also wanted to take the war closer to the nation's capital in Washington, D.C. He hoped that this would throw the Union and President Abraham Lincoln's administration into a state of confusion. This would not only give the Confederates a political victory, but fighting on Northern soil could also be a military victory. If Washington, D.C., was threatened, Lincoln would have to pull Union troops from other parts of the country to protect the capital. This could improve Confederate chances of winning the war.

CSA president Davis believed that if his armies could win an important victory on Northern soil, then France and Great Britain would recognize the Confederacy as a nation and possibly come to their aid, forcing the North to end the war.

✵ *Union general Joseph Hooker was known as "Fighting Joe." He commanded the Army of the Potomac from December 1862 to May 1863.*

**G**eneral Joseph Hooker was commander of the Union army. Hooker's army had the supplies that the South did not, but he was uncertain over where and how to do battle with the Confederates. He also incorrectly believed that Southern forces outnumbered his own by 2 to 1.

Hooker was also indecisive about whether he should attack Richmond, Virginia, the capital of the Confederate government, or take his battle directly

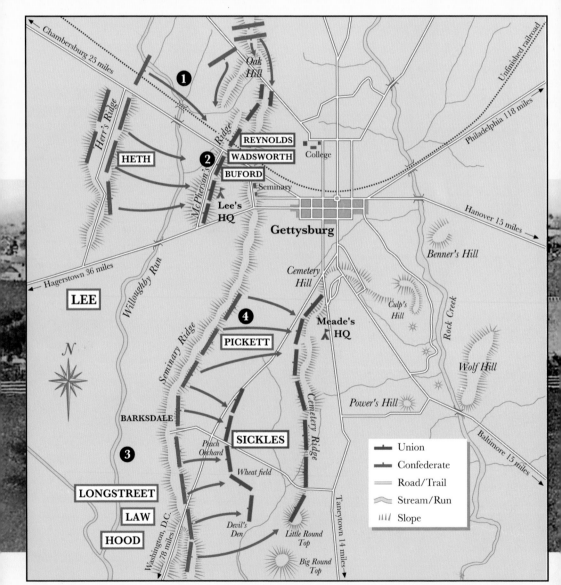

★ *The Battle of Gettysburg, July 1–3, 1863, was made up of several smaller fights between Union and Confederate forces. The most important of these were* (1) *the initial fight between Generals Heth and Buford on July 1 (which resulted in the death of Union general Reynolds at McPherson's Ridge)* (2), *the July 2 battle between Generals Longstreet and Sickles in the fight to break the Union line* (3), *and Pickett's charge on July 3, which led to the death of 6,500 Confederates* (4).

to General Lee. Because of General Hooker's lack of strong action, President Lincoln replaced him as commander of the Union army with General George Meade.

Unlike Hooker, General Lee was brimming with confidence. In early May he had defeated Hooker's army at the Battle of Chancellorsville in Virginia. Lee believed his army was capable of anything, and he was determined to defeat the Union army on their home ground—even though he had no fixed plan as to where the battle would take place.

Confederate General J.E.B. Stuart was also eager for battle. His reputation as

★ **Gen. J.E.B. Stuart**

*Confederate general J.E.B. Stuart was only twenty-eight at the start of the war. He went on to become one of the most important cavalry commanders of the war.*

the greatest cavalry commander in the world had been severely hurt by his defeat at the Battle of Brandy Station in Virginia on June 9, 1863. Fighting the Union army on its home ground, and winning, would restore his reputation.

No one on either the Confederate or the Union side intended to stage a major battle at Gettysburg. The armies met there more by accident than anything else. However, events soon unfolded that ensured Gettysburg would become one of the most famous battles in American history.

★ *Gettysburg was a small, quiet town that suddenly became the place where a battle would decide the fate of a nation.*

# THE BATTLE OF GETTYSBURG
## Spilled Blood on Sacred Ground

JUNE 30, 1863. UNION GENERAL JOHN BUFORD TRAVELED TO GETTYSBURG WITH HIS 1ST DIVISION CAVALRY CORPS.

IF WE HOLD GETTYSBURG WE CAN CONTROL THE AREA AND KEEP THE CONFEDERATES AT BAY.

THE CONFEDERATES ARE COMING FROM THE WEST! THEY'VE BEEN SCOUTING THE TOWN.

FORM UP!

SEND OUT A SCOUTING PARTY. I WANT TO KNOW THE STRENGTH OF THE CONFEDERATE FORCES.

THE MEN OF THE CAVALRY CORPS FORMED UP ON MCPHERSON'S RIDGE. TEAMS OF SKIRMISHERS COVERED THE CHAMBERSBURG ROAD.

WE'LL NEED OUR SLEEP IF WE'RE TO FIGHT IN THE MORNING.

THE CONFEDERATE FORCES ARE NINE MILES AWAY, SIR.

THEY'RE JUST FORAGERS. WE'RE IN NO DANGER.

BUT REPORTS SUGGEST THAT CONFEDERATE FORCES ARE MASSING ALL AROUND US.

THEN WE'RE GOING TO NEED REINFORCEMENTS.

JUNE 30, 1863. CONFEDERATE GENERAL JAMES J. PETTIGREW SAW THE UNION TROOPS ENTERING GETTYSBURG.

WITHDRAW THE MEN. OUR ORDERS ARE NOT TO ENGAGE THE ENEMY.

YES, SIR!

THERE'S TALK OF SHOES IN THE TOWN, SIR. THE MEN CERTAINLY NEED THEM.

VERY WELL, PETTIGREW. MOST OF THE UNION FORCES ARE AT MIDDLEBURG.

GENERAL HILL, WE SAW SOME UNION SOLDIERS ENTERING THE TOWN, BUT I'M SURE IT WAS JUST THE LOCAL MILITIA.

LET'S ATTACK GETTYSBURG IN THE MORNING AND OCCUPY THE TOWN.

VERY WELL. GENERAL HETH MUST PROCEED AT FIRST LIGHT.

JULY 1, 1863. 5:15 A.M. GENERAL HETH'S INFANTRY TRAVELED EAST ALONG THE CHAMBERSBURG ROAD, HEADING TOWARD GETTYSBURG.

GENERAL HETH SPREAD HIS MEN FROM NORTH TO SOUTH, ACROSS THE MAIN ROAD THAT LED INTO THE TOWN.

GENERAL BUFORD'S CAVALRY CORPS WATCHED THEM COME.

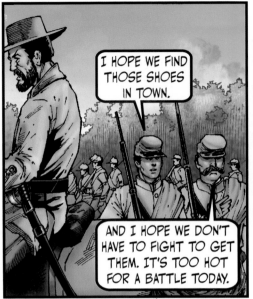

I HOPE WE FIND THOSE SHOES IN TOWN.

AND I HOPE WE DON'T HAVE TO FIGHT TO GET THEM. IT'S TOO HOT FOR A BATTLE TODAY.

5:30 A.M.

FIRE!

UNION LIEUTENANT MARCELLUS JONES IDENTIFIED THE ENEMY COMING TOWARD HIS TROOPS.

LIEUTENANT JONES GAVE THE COMMAND FOR THE FIRST SHOTS TO BE FIRED AT GETTYSBURG. THE PICKET'S FIRST TARGET WAS A MOUNTED CONFEDERATE OFFICER.

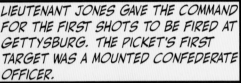

KRAK! KRAK!

KRAK! KLIK! KRAK!

AARGH!

HE'S BEEN SHOT! SIR!

PREPARE TO RETURN FIRE ...

EMMITSBURG, 11 MILES FROM GETTYSBURG. UNION MAJOR GENERAL JOHN F. REYNOLDS WAS THE FIRST TO HEAR OF THE SITUATION AT GETTYSBURG.

DISPATCHES FROM GENERAL BUFORD, SIR.

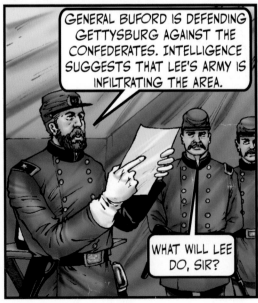

GENERAL BUFORD IS DEFENDING GETTYSBURG AGAINST THE CONFEDERATES. INTELLIGENCE SUGGESTS THAT LEE'S ARMY IS INFILTRATING THE AREA.

WHAT WILL LEE DO, SIR?

HE COULD ATTACK WASHINGTON, OR PURSUE OUR ARMIES FOR A FULL-SCALE BATTLE. YET HE MIGHT EVEN CONVERGE HIS TROOPS ON GETTYSBURG. SEND BUFORD'S DISPATCHES AND MY REPORT TO GENERAL MEADE.

TWENTY-FOUR MILES SOUTH OF GETTYSBURG...

...GENERAL GEORGE MEADE WAS THE NEWLY APPOINTED COMMANDER OF THE UNION FORCES.

THE GROUND AT EMMITSBURG OFFERS US NO ADVANTAGE IF WE FIGHT THERE ...

...WE COULD RETREAT AND CHOOSE OUR OWN GROUND, BUT PRESIDENT LINCOLN WANTS OUR ARMIES TO BE AGGRESSIVE!

I, XI, AND III CORPS MUST MAKE HASTE TO GETTYSBURG.

WE'VE ONLY GAINED A FEW HUNDRED YARDS. HOW LONG HAVE WE BEEN HERE?

A COUPLE OF HOURS...

...AND ALL FOR A PAIR OF SHOES!

UNDER HUGE PRESSURE FROM THE CONFEDERATE FORCES, THE UNION CAVALRY CORPS WERE SLOWLY RETREATING.

8:00 A.M. TWO OF GENERAL HETH'S LEAD BRIGADES HAD MADE IT TO WILLOUGHBY RUN, WHERE THEY COULD CROSS THE STREAM AND ATTACK THE UNION FORCES ON McPHERSON'S RIDGE.

BUFORD'S SKIRMISHERS KEPT UP A STEADY STREAM OF FIRE ON THE ADVANCING CONFEDERATE INFANTRY.

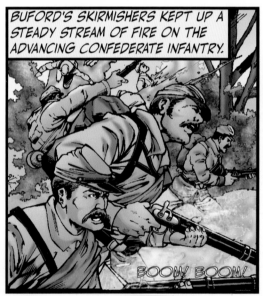

THE CONFEDERATE SOLDIERS RALLIED.

AS THEY CROSSED THE ROUGH TERRAIN, THE CONFEDERATES SPLIT INTO TWO FIGHTING FORCES.

BELMONT SCHOOLHOUSE RIDGE. THE CONFEDERATES HEARD THE UNION GUNS ON McPHERSON'S RIDGE AND RETURNED FIRE.

CONFEDERATE AND UNION ARTILLERY FIRED ON EACH OTHER'S POSITIONS.

FOR AN HOUR, THE SOUND OF HEAVY GUNFIRE MIXED WITH THE CRACKLE OF MUSKET AND CARBINE FIRE.

BOMBARDED BY HEAVY GUNFIRE, THE UNION FORCES RETREATED.

9:00 A.M. THE SEMINARY, GENERAL BUFORD'S HEADQUARTERS.

BUFORD SAW HIS TROOPS RETREATING. HE THEN SPOTTED GENERAL REYNOLDS RIDING TOWARD HIM.

REINFORCEMENTS ARE COMING. CAN YOU HOLD OFF THE CONFEDERATES UNTIL THEY REACH YOU?

THE DEVIL'S TO PAY! *

* BALLOONS COLORED BLUE REPRESENT ACTUAL SPOKEN DIALOGUE.

BUFORD COULD SEE THAT THE CONFEDERATES WERE GAINING GROUND ON McPHERSON'S RIDGE.

I RECKON I CAN!

THOUSANDS OF SOLDIERS FROM BOTH SIDES BEGAN TO ARRIVE AT GETTYSBURG.

REYNOLDS AND HIS GROUP MET BRIGADIER GENERAL JAMES WADSWORTH AND HIS REINFORCEMENTS, EAST OF McPHERSON'S RIDGE.

THERE'S HEAVY FIRE TO THE WEST!

IRON BRIGADE, TO THE WEST AND FORM UP!

THE REBS ARE THICKER 'N BLACKBERRIES AHEAD!

YOU HEARD HIM, MEN!

THE CONFEDERATES MADE STRONG ADVANCES AGAINST GENERAL BUFORD'S TROOPS.

... HOWEVER, MORE THAN 500 CONFEDERATE INFANTRYMEN WERE WAITING IN A RAILROAD CUT SOUTH OF McPHERSON'S RIDGE.

BUT UNION INFANTRY HURRIED INTO POSITION, DETERMINED TO SUPPORT THE ARTILLERY GUNFIRE ...

THEY WERE READY TO AMBUSH UNION MAJOR JAMES HALL'S ARTILLERY BELOW THE RIDGE.

KRAK!
KRAK!

FIRE!

NORTH OF THE PIKE, MEN! WE'LL SUPPORT GENERAL HALL'S GUNS!

BOOM!

HALL WHEELED HIS GUNS AND FIRED WITH DEADLY EFFECT.

GENERAL BUFORD NEEDS HELP HERE! RE-FORM AND SUPPORT HIM!

THE UNION WAS SOON IN POSITION ON THE EASTERN SLOPE OF McPHERSON'S RIDGE.

YESSIR, GENERAL WADSWORTH!

CAUGHT IN A BRUTAL CROSSFIRE, HALL'S GUNS BEGAN TO WITHDRAW.

WADSWORTH'S MEN FOUND THEMSELVES IN A VICIOUS FIREFIGHT, BEFORE THEY COULD HELP HALL'S GUNS.

KRAK! KRAK! KLIK! KRAK!

234 OUT OF 375 OF WADSWORTH'S MEN DIED IN THE FIGHT.

FORWARD MEN, FORWARD, FOR GOD'S SAKE, AND DRIVE THOSE FELLOWS OUT OF THOSE WOODS!

REYNOLDS AGAIN RALLIED HIS MEN TO DRIVE THE CONFEDERATES OUT OF THE WOODS BETWEEN McPHERSON'S RIDGE AND SEMINARY RIDGE.

DESPITE THE UNION FORCES' BEST EFFORTS, THE CONFEDERATES COULD NOT BE MADE TO WITHDRAW.

BUT HE WAS STRUCK AND KILLED BY A CONFEDERATE SHARPSHOOTER'S BULLET.

SOME SOLDIERS HAD NO IDEA WHAT WAS GOING ON AROUND THEM.

THERE'S TOO MANY OF THEM TO BE THE LOCAL MILITIA!

WHERE ARE ALL THESE YANKS COMING FROM?

KRAK! KRAK!

T'AIN'T NO MILITIA! IT'S THE ARMY OF THE POTOMAC!

BY THE END OF THE DAY'S FIGHTING, CONFEDERATE FORCES HAD GAINED GROUND AT GETTYSBURG. THEY HAD ALSO BENEFITED FROM THE ARRIVAL OF FRESH TROOPS. YET UNION FORCES HAD DECIMATED CONFEDERATE TROOPS IN THE RAILROAD CUT AND CONTINUED TO HOLD SOME OF THE HIGH GROUND.

CONFEDERATE COMMANDER, GENERAL LEE, WAS CONCERNED BECAUSE LIEUTENANT GENERAL LONGSTREET'S FORCES HAD STILL NOT ARRIVED.

HAD I NOT BETTER ATTACK?

I AM NOT PREPARED TO BRING ON A GENERAL ENGAGEMENT TODAY.

GENERAL LEE LATER REVERSED THIS DECISION.

GENERAL EWELL MUST TAKE THE HIGH GROUND AT SEMINARY RIDGE, IF AT ALL PRACTICABLE.

WHEN EWELL RECEIVED THE ORDER, HE BELIEVED IT COULD NOT BE ACCOMPLISHED, AND CHOSE TO IGNORE IT.

EWELL LATER MET WITH LEE. HE PROPOSED A NEW OBJECTIVE, WHICH LEE AGREED TO.

AT FIRST LIGHT, WE SHOULD ATTACK THE UNION FORCES FROM BEHIND, AT CULP'S HILL, AND GAIN THE HIGH GROUND THAT WAY.

LEE, WHO HAD BEEN ILL FOR SOME TIME, LATER CHANGED HIS MIND.

CULP'S HILL IS NO USE. UNION FORCES WOULD NEVER ALLOW AN ATTACK TO THE REAR OF THEIR LINE.

UNION COMMANDER MEADE ARRIVED LATE ON THE NIGHT OF JULY 1.

WE'VE SUFFERED 8,500 DEAD.

THE CONFEDERATES DID NOT WITHDRAW. WE ARE RETREATING...

...AND ONLY BUFORD HELD HIS GROUND.

JULY 2, DAWN. GENERALS MEADE AND OLIVER HOWARD MADE PLANS ...

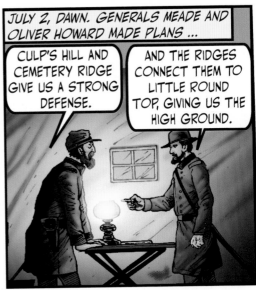

CULP'S HILL AND CEMETERY RIDGE GIVE US A STRONG DEFENSE.

AND THE RIDGES CONNECT THEM TO LITTLE ROUND TOP, GIVING US THE HIGH GROUND.

THE LINE RUNS SOUTH FROM CEMETERY RIDGE TO BIG ROUND TOP.

THE CONFEDERATES WILL ATTACK FROM SEMINARY RIDGE TO THE WEST. WE MUST CONTROL THE EMMITSBURG ROAD.

GENERAL LEE MET WITH GENERALS HOOD, HILL, AND HETH. GENERAL LONGSTREET HAD ALSO FINALLY ARRIVED.

LONGSTREET, YOU WILL ATTACK THE UNION LEFT FLANK FROM THE SOUTH AND PUSH THEM NORTH.

I DISAGREE, SIR.

LONGSTREET PREFERRED TO GO AROUND THE UNION TROOPS, BUT LEE INSISTED ON HIS PLAN. LATER, MAJOR GENERAL LAFAYETTE McLAWS JOINED LEE.

DEPLOY YOUR MEN BETWEEN THE ROUND TOP HILLS AND EMMITSBURG ROAD.

GENERAL LEE THEN MET WITH GENERAL EWELL.

WHEN YOU HEAR LONGSTREET'S GUNS, PRESS THE UNION RIGHT FLANK. MAKE A FULL ASSAULT IF YOU CAN.

WHERE ARE CAPTAIN JOHNSON'S REPORTS OF THE ENEMY'S POSITION?

AND WHY AREN'T YOU MOVING FORWARD, LONGSTREET?

JOHNSON HASN'T RETURNED FROM HIS SCOUTING MISSION, AND WE DON'T HAVE ALL OF OUR OFFICERS, SIR.

WE SHOULD ONLY ATTACK WHEN EVERYTHING IS IN PLACE.

I THOUGHT WE HAD ORDERS? AREN'T WE GOING TO FIGHT TODAY?

I DON'T CARE IF WE DON'T. THE WHOLE UNION ARMY'S OUT THERE!

EARLY AFTERNOON. THE CONFEDERATE ARMY WAS ADVANCING ON THE UNION FORCES ON HERR'S RIDGE.

WE CAN'T TAKE THIS ROUTE. THE UNION ARMY CAN SEE US!

RETREAT AND TRY TO FIND A SAFER ROUTE, GENERAL KERSHAW.

WHAT'S GOING ON? WE'RE MARCHING BACK TO WHERE WE STARTED!

WE'RE GOING TO BE MARCHING ALL DAY AT THIS RATE.

1:00 P.M. GENERAL J.E.B. STUART AND THE CONFEDERATE CAVALRY ARRIVED IN GETTYSBURG.

I HAVE NOT HEARD A WORD FROM YOU FOR DAYS, STUART.

AND YOU ARE SUPPOSED TO BE THE EYES AND EARS OF MY ARMY.

WE'VE BEEN FIGHTING TO PROTECT OUR SUPPLY WAGONS. MY MEN CANNOT FIGHT AGAIN TODAY!

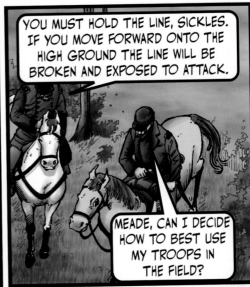
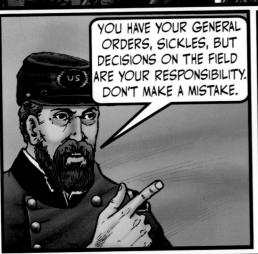
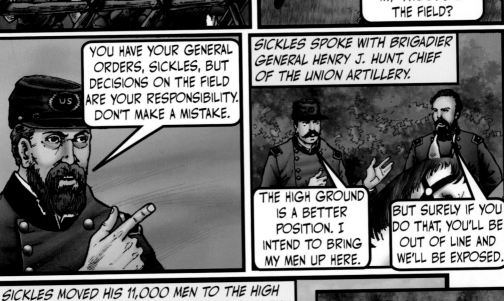

TWO OF CONFEDERATE GENERAL LONGSTREET'S INFANTRY DIVISIONS HEADED UP THE EMMITSBURG ROAD, UNDER THE COMMAND OF GENERALS JOHN HOOD AND EVANDER LAW.

WE'RE TOO EXPOSED HERE, LAW! WE NEED TO GET OFF THIS ROAD.

HOOD ASKED LONGSTREET IF HE COULD TAKE HIS MEN SOUTH AND ATTACK THE UNION LINE FROM THE REAR AT BIG ROUND TOP?

GENERAL LEE'S ORDERS ARE TO ATTACK UP THE EMMITSBURG ROAD.

GET OFF THE ROAD, MEN, BUT CONTINUE NORTH AS BEST YOU CAN WITHOUT BEING SEEN.

LAW DID HIS BEST TO FOLLOW HOOD'S LEAD, BUT MOVED TOO FAR FROM THE EMMITSBURG ROAD. HE FOUND HIMSELF IN DEVIL'S DEN.

THEN HOOD WAS SHOT AND HE PASSED OVER COMMAND TO GENERAL LAW.

LAW KNEW THAT HIS MEN WERE WALKING INTO GREAT DANGER, BUT HE HADN'T THE POWER TO STOP IT.

THIS IS HELL!

THIS ISN'T WAR! IT'S A RAMPAGE!

FIRE!

KRAK! BOOM! KRAK!

THE CONFEDERATES KEPT PUSHING FORWARD, BUT WERE NO MATCH FOR THE UNION FIREPOWER. EVENTUALLY, THEY WERE FORCED TO RETREAT.

THEY FOUGHT WITHOUT SUPPORT FOR AN HOUR AND A HALF.

BRIGADIER GENERAL GOUVERNEUR WARREN WAS CHIEF ENGINEER TO THE ARMY OF THE POTOMAC. FROM HIS POSITION, HIGH ON LITTLE ROUND TOP, HE COULD SEE THE UNION DEFENSES.

SOUTH OF LITTLE ROUND TOP, THE CONFEDERATES WERE ATTACKING BIG ROUND TOP.

WITH SUPPORT COMING FROM ALL SIDES, THE CONFEDERATES WERE MASSING AROUND BIG ROUND TOP.

FROM HIS POSITION ON BIG ROUND TOP, CONFEDERATE COLONEL WILLIAM OATES ALSO REALIZED THE IMPORTANCE OF LITTLE ROUND TOP.

WE MUST HOLD THAT HILL! I NEED ARTILLERY REINFORCEMENTS!

THE CONFEDERATE INFANTRY ON BIG ROUND TOP RESPONDED TO THE PUNISHING FIRE FROM WARREN'S UNION ARTILLERY.

THE CONFEDERATES ARE MASSING TO THE SOUTH. WE MUST HOLD LITTLE ROUND TOP BEFORE THEY TAKE THE ADVANTAGE.

WHOEVER COMMANDS LITTLE ROUND TOP COMMANDS THE FIELD OF BATTLE!

GENERAL SYKES, I HAVE RE-QUESTED REINFORCEMENTS FROM GENERAL MEADE, BUT ...

...WE NEED TO TAKE LITTLE ROUND TOP. NOW!

UNION COLONEL STRONG VINCENT WAS CALLED UPON FOR BRIGADIER GENERAL WARREN'S REINFORCEMENTS.

COLONEL VINCENT, GENERAL SYKES WANTS A BRIGADE AT THE TOP OF LITTLE ROUND TOP.

THEN WHAT ARE WE WAITING FOR?

CHARGE!

20TH MAINE TO THE SOUTHERN FACE!

YOU MEN TO THE WESTERN SLOPE! NOW!

UNION COLONEL JOSHUA CHAMBERLAIN, COMMANDER OF THE 20TH MAINE, REALIZED THAT THE CONFEDERATES WERE ATTACKING ON TWO SIDES.

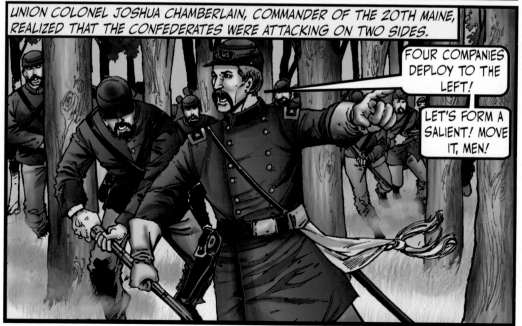

FOUR COMPANIES DEPLOY TO THE LEFT!

LET'S FORM A SALIENT! MOVE IT, MEN!

TWO TEXAS REGIMENTS POUNDED THE WESTERN SLOPES OF LITTLE ROUND TOP.

AAARGH! DON'T GIVE AN INCH, MEN!

EVEN AS COLONEL STRONG VINCENT WAS DYING, HE CONTINUED TO RALLY HIS MEN.

UNION GENERAL WARREN HAD ROUNDED UP ALL THE TROOPS HE COULD.

ON THE WESTERN SLOPES OF LITTLE ROUND TOP, CHARLES HAZLETT'S UNION ARTILLERYMEN WERE TAKING FIRE FROM SNIPERS IN DEVIL'S DEN, BELOW THEM.

UNION BRIGADIER GENERAL STEVEN H. WEED ARRIVED ON LITTLE ROUND TOP. HE WAS GREETED BY LIEUTENANT HAZLETT.

THE BATTLE IS ALL BUT OVER, GENERAL. OUR MEN ARE DYING.

A SECOND SNIPER TOOK AIM AND SHOT HAZLETT THROUGH THE HEAD, KILLING HIM INSTANTLY.

AS WEED TURNED TO HIS MEN A CONFEDERATE SNIPER SHOT HIM.

CHARGE!

KRAK! KRAK! KRAK!

HOLD YOUR GROUND!

THE UNION FORCES WERE ALMOST FACING DEFEAT IN THE WHEAT FIELD.

WITHDRAW!

UNION REINFORCEMENTS REPELLED THE ENEMY, WHO RETREATED BACK THROUGH THE WHEAT FIELD.

MORE CONFEDERATE REINFORCEMENTS ARRIVED, UNDER HEAVY FIRE FROM UNION ARTILLERY.

IN THE WHEAT FIELD, BOTH FORCES ATTACKED AND COUNTERATTACKED.

FINALLY, MORE UNION REINFORCEMENTS FORCED THE CONFEDERATES BACK AGAIN INTO THE WOODS.

THE CONFEDERATES MADE A COUNTEROFFENSIVE.

UNION COLONEL JACOB B. SWEITZER'S MEN WERE ON HAND ONCE AGAIN TO STOP THE CONFEDERATE COUNTEROFFENSIVE.

SWEITZER'S CORPS SOON FOUND ITSELF FIGHTING ON TWO FRONTS.

WITHDRAW!

RETREAT!

THEY RETREATED TO THE UNION DEFENSES AT LITTLE ROUND TOP ...

... AND THEY PASSED THROUGH THE LINES AND CLOSED RANKS.

THE PENNSYLVANIAN REGIMENT, LED BY BRIGADIER GENERAL SAMUEL CRAWFORD, FINALLY PUNCHED OUT THE LAST OF THE CONFEDERATE TROOPS THAT THEY HAD BEEN SKIRMISHING WITH ALL DAY.

LEE'S ORDERS HAD ALSO INCLUDED ATTACKING CEMETERY RIDGE. THERE, THE CONFEDERATES WERE BOMBARDED BY UNION FIRE, BUT THEY STILL MADE PROGRESS.

BOOM! BOOM! KRAK!

THE UNION HAD FORMED A SALIENT AROUND THE PEACH ORCHARD, WHICH WAS UNDER ATTACK FROM CONFEDERATE INFANTRY.

CONFEDERATES UNDER BRIGADIER GENERAL CADMUS WILCOX OVERRAN THE UNION ARTILLERY POSITION IN THE PEACH ORCHARD.

WE GOT 'EM!

WE HAD THE YANKEES RUNNING SCARED!

THE UNION ARMY BATTLED ON ...

... BUT COULD NOT HOLD THE CONFEDERATES WITHOUT REINFORCEMENTS.

TWO BRIGADES WITHDREW UNDER FIRE.

THE LAST OF THE NORTHERN ARMY WAS DRIVEN BACK BY CONFEDERATE INFANTRY AND ARTILLERY.

THE BATTLE RAGED BETWEEN THE EMMITSBURG ROAD AND CEMETERY RIDGE. THE UNION FORCES WERE SPLINTERED BY THE MIGHT OF THE SOUTHERN FORCES.

GENERAL WINFIELD SCOTT HANCOCK WAS PUT IN CHARGE OF THE UNION II CORPS WHEN MAJOR GENERAL JOHN REYNOLDS DIED IN BATTLE THE PREVIOUS DAY.

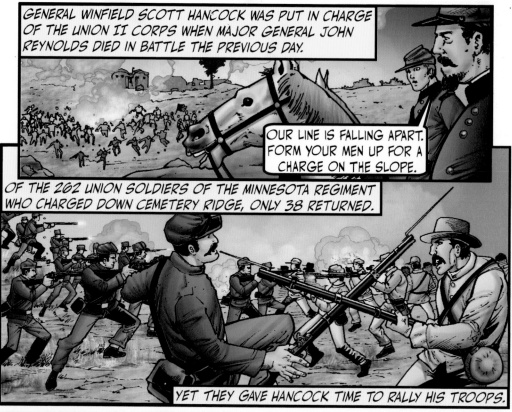

OUR LINE IS FALLING APART. FORM YOUR MEN UP FOR A CHARGE ON THE SLOPE.

OF THE 262 UNION SOLDIERS OF THE MINNESOTA REGIMENT WHO CHARGED DOWN CEMETERY RIDGE, ONLY 38 RETURNED.

YET THEY GAVE HANCOCK TIME TO RALLY HIS TROOPS.

UNDER GENERAL HANCOCK'S COMMAND, THE UNION FORCES RALLIED AND STALLED THE CONFEDERATES IN THEIR ATTACK.

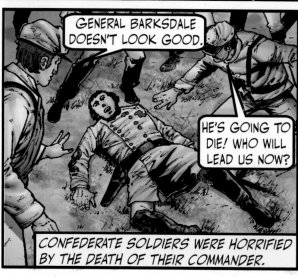

GENERAL BARKSDALE DOESN'T LOOK GOOD.

HE'S GOING TO DIE! WHO WILL LEAD US NOW?

CONFEDERATE SOLDIERS WERE HORRIFIED BY THE DEATH OF THEIR COMMANDER.

7:30 P.M. AFTER THEIR VICTORY, THE UNION FORCES WITHDREW TO CEMETERY RIDGE.

THE CONFEDERATES RETREATED TO SEMINARY RIDGE.

EARLIER, AT 4:00 P.M. ON BENNER'S HILL. A CONFEDERATE ARTILLERY CORPS FORMED UP TO THE NORTHEAST OF THE BATTLEFIELD.

THE CONFEDERATE ARTILLERY SHELLED CULP'S HILL AND CEMETERY HILL FOR TWO HOURS.

WHEN THE SHELLING STOPPED, GENERAL EWELL MOVED HIS MEN, DESPITE IT BEING CONTRARY TO GENERAL LEE'S ORDERS.

GENERAL JOHNSON, RALLY YOUR MEN, WE WILL ATTACK CULP'S HILL!

HOW FAR IS IT? THIS DOESN'T FEEL LIKE AN ATTACK, MORE LIKE A ROUTE MARCH!

AT THIS RATE THERE WON'T BE MUCH LIGHT LEFT BY THE TIME WE GET TO ATTACKING.

JOHNSON'S MEN ATTACKED UNDER FIRE. UNION GENERALS GREENE AND ROBINSON HAD DUG IN THEIR TROOPS IN DEFENSE OF THE CONFEDERATE ARMY'S SUPERIOR NUMBERS.

KRAK! KRAK! KRAK!

TO THE RIGHT OF THE UNION POSITION, CONFEDERATE GENERAL GEORGE H. STEUART STUMBLED UPON EMPTY TRENCHES. THERE WAS A CHANCE OF ROUTING THE UNION FORCES ON CULP'S HILL.

SEND FOR REINFORCEMENTS. THIS SIDE IS UNDEFENDED!

LATER...

NO ONE SEEMS TO BE COMING TO HELP US. NOW IT'S TOO DARK TO ATTACK!

THAT NIGHT, MEADE MET WITH HIS GENERALS.

WE HAVE TAKEN HEAVY LOSSES. GENERAL ZOOK AND COMMANDERS VINCENT, WEED, AND WILLARD ARE ALL DEAD.

THE TERRAIN HAS BEEN KIND TO US, GENERAL WILLIAMS. WE HELD THE HIGH GROUND FROM THE BEGINNING, AND WE TOOK UP A STRONG DEFENSIVE LINE.

BUT WE HAVE NOT WON THIS BATTLE YET!

BUT OUR LINE HAS HELD WELL AGAINST THE CONFEDERATE ARMY. THEIR NUMBERS ARE VAST!

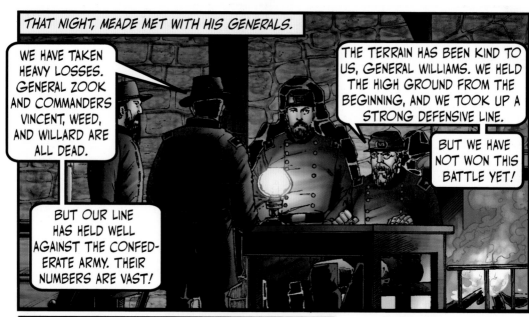

WE WILL CONTINUE TO DEFEND AND SUPPORT THE LINE. MAKE THE CONFEDERATES COME TO US!

ANYTHING ELSE? GENERAL WILLIAMS?

VERY WELL, WILLIAMS. SEND FRESH TROOPS IN BEFORE FIRST LIGHT. WE SHALL BE THE WINNERS!

I SUGGEST WE ATTACK CULP'S HILL. THE BATTLE IS OVER FOR TODAY, BUT IT IS A TIE IN THE DARK.

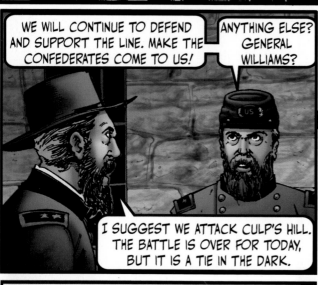

TOMORROW WE MUST BREAK THE UNION LINE!

THAT NIGHT, LEE AND HIS GENERALS DISCUSSED PLANS FOR THE FOLLOWING DAY.

WE HAVE ATTACKED TO THE RIGHT AND TO THE LEFT, AND WE HAVE REACHED CULP'S HILL.

YET WE HOLD THE SAME GROUND TODAY AS WE DID YESTERDAY AND WE HAVE LOST MANY MEN.

GENERAL LONGSTREET WORKED MOST OF THE NIGHT ON A PLAN OF ATTACK FOR THE NEXT DAY.

JULY 3, BEFORE DAWN.

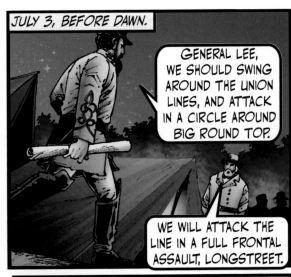

GENERAL LEE, WE SHOULD SWING AROUND THE UNION LINES, AND ATTACK IN A CIRCLE AROUND BIG ROUND TOP.

WE WILL ATTACK THE LINE IN A FULL FRONTAL ASSAULT, LONGSTREET.

MAJOR GENERAL PICKETT'S DIVISION IS FRESH. IF ANYONE CAN CRACK THE UNION LINE, THEY CAN!

WE'LL SOFTEN THE LINE WITH AN ARTILLERY ATTACK.

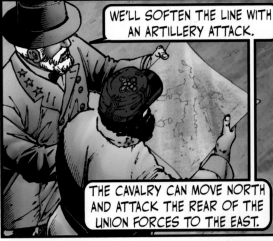

THE CAVALRY CAN MOVE NORTH AND ATTACK THE REAR OF THE UNION FORCES TO THE EAST.

ONCE AGAIN, LONGSTREET DISAGREED WITH LEE.

GENERAL, IT IS MY OPINION THAT NO FIFTEEN THOUSAND MEN EVER ARRANGED FOR BATTLE CAN TAKE THAT POSITION.

AT SEMINARY RIDGE, CONFEDERATE BRIGADIER GENERAL JAMES J. PETTIGREW WAS LEFT IN COMMAND OF GENERAL HETH'S FORCES. HE WAS WORRIED ABOUT THE NEXT DAY.

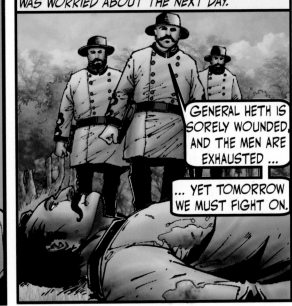

GENERAL HETH IS SORELY WOUNDED, AND THE MEN ARE EXHAUSTED ...

... YET TOMORROW WE MUST FIGHT ON.

4:30 A.M. UNION ARTILLERY BLASTED THE CONFEDERATE FORCES WAITING ON CULP'S HILL.

GENERAL WILLIAMS'S STRATEGY WORKED.

WE WILL DRIVE THE SOUTHERNERS OUT. OR AT THE VERY LEAST KEEP THEM HOLED UP WHILE WE MOVE IN AND TAKE THEM OUT.

AT THE SAME TIME, CONFEDERATE BRIGADIER GENERAL JAMES WALKER WAS BRINGING IN MORE CONFEDERATE INFANTRY TO SUPPORT STEUART'S REQUEST FOR REINFORCEMENTS.

HOWEVER, GENERAL WALKER MET WITH RESISTANCE FROM UNION ARTILLERY ON THE EASTERN SLOPES OF CULP'S HILL.

9:00 A.M. GENERAL WALKER'S CONFEDERATE FORCES WERE STOPPED IN THEIR TRACKS, AND UNABLE TO HELP STEUART'S MEN.

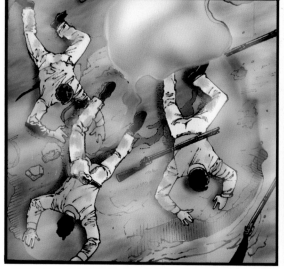

10:10 A.M. GENERAL STEUART HAD BEEN GIVEN ORDERS TO ATTACK, BUT WALKER'S REINFORCEMENTS HAD NOT REACHED HIM.

WE CAN'T! IT'LL BE A DISASTER!

STEUART WAS RIGHT. HIS TROOPS WERE DECIMATED.

9:45 A.M. AT THE SAME TIME AS STEUART'S ORDERS WERE GIVEN, UNION FORCES UNDER COLONEL CHARLES MUDGE WERE ORDERED TO ATTACK THE BREASTWORKS NEAR SPANGLER'S SPRING.

IT'S MURDER, BUT IT'S THE ORDER. FORWARD, DOUBLE QUICK.

THE UNION FORCES WERE ATTACKED WHILE CROSSING AN OPEN MEADOW. THE INFANTRY WAS TORN APART.

KRAK! KRAK! KRAK!

SOME OF THE UNION SOLDIERS MADE IT AS FAR AS THE BREASTWORKS.

COLONEL MUDGE WAS NOT ONE OF THEM.

FALL BACK, MEN!

11:45 A.M. THE UNION FORCES WERE DOWN TO HALF STRENGTH. THE BATTLE WAS LOST, AND THE SURVIVORS FELL BACK.

ON SEMINARY RIDGE, CONFEDERATE GENERAL PETTIGREW'S FORCES FORMED UP IN THE TREE LINE.

FORM UP, MEN!

THE CONFEDERATES PREPARED FOR A MASSED ASSAULT.

IT INCLUDED 50 REGIMENTS OF SOLDIERS THAT REPRESENTED SIX DIFFERENT CONFEDERATE STATES.

SEVENTY-FIVE GUNS WERE RANGED ALONG THE STRETCH BETWEEN THE PEACH ORCHARD AND SPANGLER'S WOOD.

THESE SUPPORT WEAPONS COVERED THREE-QUARTERS OF A MILE OF GROUND.

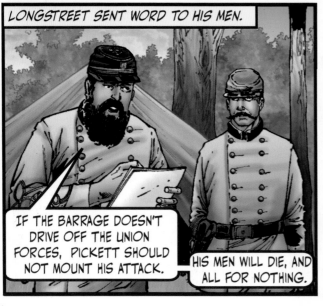

LONGSTREET SENT WORD TO HIS MEN.

IF THE BARRAGE DOESN'T DRIVE OFF THE UNION FORCES, PICKETT SHOULD NOT MOUNT HIS ATTACK.

HIS MEN WILL DIE, AND ALL FOR NOTHING.

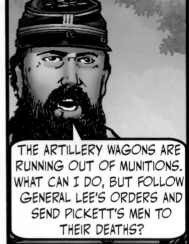

HE SOON GOT BACK AN ANSWER.

THE ARTILLERY WAGONS ARE RUNNING OUT OF MUNITIONS. WHAT CAN I DO, BUT FOLLOW GENERAL LEE'S ORDERS AND SEND PICKETT'S MEN TO THEIR DEATHS?

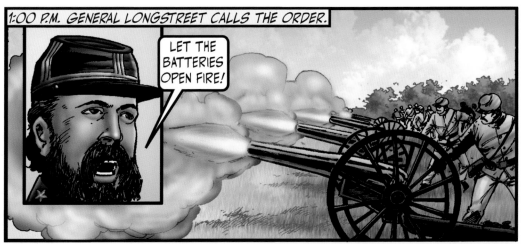

LET THE BATTERIES OPEN FIRE!

THE AIM OF THE CONFEDERATE GUNS WAS POOR. INSTEAD OF HITTING THE UNION LINE ON SEMINARY RIDGE, THE GUNS FIRED ON GENERAL MEADE'S HEADQUARTERS.

THERE WERE GREATER LOSSES AMONGST THE UNION ARTILLERY TO THE REAR OF THE LINE.

2:50 P.M.

GUNNERS, WITHDRAW!

CONFEDERATE COLONEL E. PORTER ALEXANDER, WHO COMMANDED THE CANNON FIRE, WATCHED THE UNION ARTILLERY WITHDRAWAL.

THE ARTILLERY IS RETREATING. THE UNION LINE IS BROKEN.

GENERAL PICKETT MUST MAKE READY TO CHARGE!

THE NOTE FROM COLONEL ALEXANDER READ, "FOR GOD'S SAKE COME QUICK. THE 18 GUNS HAVE GONE. COME QUICK OR MY AMMUNITION WILL NOT LET ME SUPPORT YOU PROPERLY."

SHALL I ADVANCE?

GENERAL LONGSTREET, SHALL I ADVANCE?

I SHALL LEAD MY DIVISION FORWARD, SIR?

LONGSTREET SAID NOTHING. THE NOD OF HIS HEAD TO GENERAL PICKETT WAS BARELY NOTICEABLE.

LONGSTREET COULD DO NOTHING TO STOP WHAT WOULD HAPPEN. BUT THERE WAS NOTHING ELSE HE COULD DO WITHOUT ARTILLERY SUPPORT.

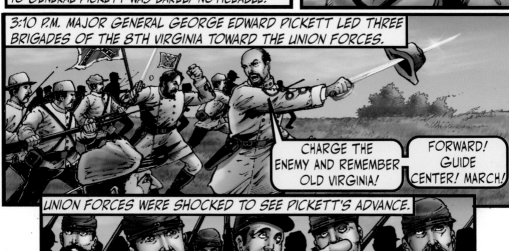

3:10 P.M. MAJOR GENERAL GEORGE EDWARD PICKETT LED THREE BRIGADES OF THE 8TH VIRGINIA TOWARD THE UNION FORCES.

CHARGE THE ENEMY AND REMEMBER OLD VIRGINIA!

FORWARD! GUIDE CENTER! MARCH!

UNION FORCES WERE SHOCKED TO SEE PICKETT'S ADVANCE.

GENERAL PETTIGREW'S MEN, WHO WERE EXHAUSTED FROM THEIR PART IN THE PREVIOUS DAYS' BATTLES, WERE THE FIRST TO BE FIRED UPON.

THEY SWERVED IN THE FACE OF THE ATTACK.

PICKETT'S MEN FOLLOWED GENERAL PETTIGREW AND TURNED AT AN ANGLE TOWARD EMMITSBURG ROAD.

WHEN THEY REACHED THEIR POSITION, UNION GUNS ON CEMETERY RIDGE AND LITTLE ROUND TOP OPENED FIRE.

PICKETT STOPPED AT BLISS BARN, AND DRESSED RANKS BEFORE CONTINUING HIS ATTACK.

THEY WERE MET WITH MORE HEAVY ARTILLERY FIRE.

THE 8TH VIRGINIA COLORS, OR FLAG, FELL FOUR TIMES IN JUST A FEW MINUTES, BUT WAS CARRIED ON.

THE CONFEDERATE SOLDIERS CHARGED THE UNION LINE.

WO-WHOOO-EY!

BUT THE UNION LINE WAS READY TO RESIST.

PICKETT'S MEN WERE FORCED TO RETREAT AT 4:00 P.M. THE FOCUS OF THEIR CHARGE BECAME KNOWN AFTERWARD AS "THE BLOODY ANGLE."

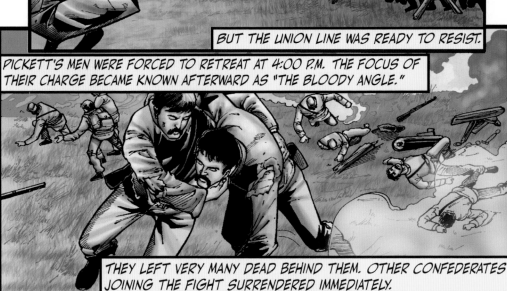

THEY LEFT VERY MANY DEAD BEHIND THEM. OTHER CONFEDERATES JOINING THE FIGHT SURRENDERED IMMEDIATELY.

ELEVEN THOUSAND MEN WALKED FOR SIXTEEN-AND-A-HALF MINUTES ACROSS A FIELD. SIXTY-FIVE HUNDRED WERE LOST.

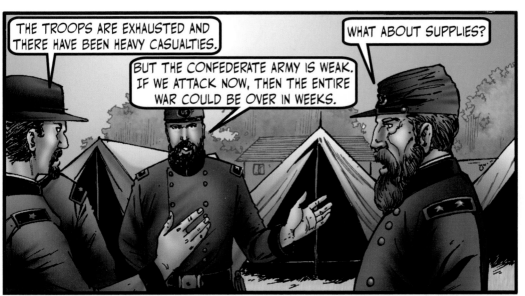

THE TROOPS ARE EXHAUSTED AND THERE HAVE BEEN HEAVY CASUALTIES.

BUT THE CONFEDERATE ARMY IS WEAK. IF WE ATTACK NOW, THEN THE ENTIRE WAR COULD BE OVER IN WEEKS.

WHAT ABOUT SUPPLIES?

WE HAVE BEEN MOVING UNITS AROUND FOR THREE DAYS. SOME OF THEM HAVE FEW SUPPLIES.

THE MEN HAVE ENDURED WAITING FOR THE ATTACK, AS WELL AS FIGHTING.

SO, MORALE IS LOW, SUPPLIES ARE SCARCE, AND CASUALTIES ARE HIGH.

I HAVE LOST GOOD MEN AND OFFICERS, AND EVEN HANCOCK IS INJURED.

WE HAVE HELD THE LINE AND THE ARMY IS INTACT. THAT IS ENOUGH.

MEADE SENT TWO UNION BRIGADES OUT IN FORCE, TO SCOUT OUT THE AREA.

THEY WATCHED THE CONFEDERATE TROOPS SLOWLY WITHDRAWING AND REPORTED BACK.

THE BATTLE WAS ALL BUT OVER, BUT IN THE LAST FEW HOURS, TWO CAVALRY ACTIONS TOOK PLACE.

AT LOTT'S FARM, J.E.B. STUART'S CONFEDERATE CAVALRY DIVISION CHARGED BRIGADIER GENERAL GEORGE ARMSTRONG CUSTER'S UNION HORSEMEN.

MEANWHILE, AT ABOUT 5:00 P.M AT THE SOUTHERN END OF THE BATTLEFIELD, MAJOR GENERAL ALFRED A. PLEASONTON'S UNION CAVALRY CHARGED THE LINES OF CONFEDERATE INFANTRY.

THE CHARGE WAS COSTLY. BOTH CAVALRY ACTIONS ACHIEVED NOTHING MORE THAN STALEMATE.

OFFICERS LIKE PLEASONTON AND CUSTER DID NOT UNDERSTAND THAT MODERN, MECHANIZED TECHNIQUES OF WAR HAD OUTMODED CAVALRY.

THE ERA OF MOUNTED WARFARE WAS AT AN END.

A SAD, SAD DAY FOR US.

TOO BAD. TOO BAD. OH, TOO BAD.

CONFEDERATE LOSSES WERE 4,637 KILLED, 12,391 WOUNDED, AND 5,846 MISSING OR CAPTURED.

THE CONFEDERACY SENT 69,700 SOLDIERS INTO BATTLE AT GETTYSBURG.

THE MATERIAL AND MEN LOST BY LEE'S ARMY OF NORTHERN VIRGINIA COULD NOT BE REPLACED.

LEE HAD TO PRESERVE HIS ARMY AT ALL COSTS TO HAVE ANY CHANCE OF WINNING THE WAR.

THE BATTLE WAS ALREADY LOST.

THE UNION ARMY SENT 95,799 SOLDIERS INTO BATTLE AT GETTYSBURG.

THE UNION ARMY HAD BEGUN TO DRAFT SOLDIERS INTO THE ARMY IN 1863. THEY USED A DRAFT TO REPLACE THE SOLDIERS THEY LOST AT GETTYSBURG.

UNION LOSSES WERE 3,149 KILLED, 14,503 WOUNDED, AND 5,161 MISSING OR CAPTURED.

JULY 4, 1863. INDEPENDENCE DAY.

THE RAIN FELL ON A GETTYSBURG THAT WAS NOW QUIET, ALMOST PEACEFUL, AFTER THE PAST THREE DAYS OF FIERCE BATTLE.

GENERAL MEADE RECEIVED A REQUEST FROM GENERAL LEE FOR AN EXCHANGE OF PRISONERS.

I CANNOT RETURN HIS MEN. THEY WILL ONLY TURN ON ME AND FIGHT ME AGAIN ON ANOTHER FIELD.

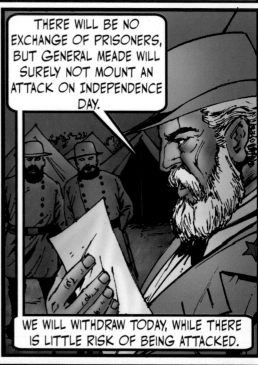

THERE WILL BE NO EXCHANGE OF PRISONERS, BUT GENERAL MEADE WILL SURELY NOT MOUNT AN ATTACK ON INDEPENDENCE DAY.

WE WILL WITHDRAW TODAY, WHILE THERE IS LITTLE RISK OF BEING ATTACKED.

IT'S OVER. WE HAVE OUR ORDERS TO WITHDRAW, BUT I DON'T KNOW HOW FAR I'LL GET.

YOU CAN ALWAYS LEAN ON ME, OLD FRIEND.

THE CONFEDERATE WITHDRAWAL CONTINUED LONG INTO THE NIGHT OF JULY 4.

THE RAIN CONTINUED TO FALL.

JULY 5, NOON.

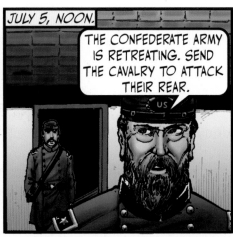

THE CONFEDERATE ARMY IS RETREATING. SEND THE CAVALRY TO ATTACK THEIR REAR.

JULY 6, 3:00 A.M. THE CAVALRY ATTACK WAS SUCCESSFUL. THE UNION FORCES CAPTURED WAGONS, TOOK PRISONERS, AND KILLED EVEN MORE CONFEDERATE MEN.

JULY 7, 1863. THE CONFEDERATE ARMY WAS UNABLE TO CROSS THE POTOMAC AT WILLIAMSPORT, BECAUSE THE RIVER WAS TOO HIGH AND THE UNION ARMY HAD DE-STROYED THE BRIDGE.

THE CONFEDERATES FORTIFIED THE AREA AND AWAITED A UNION ATTACK.

JULY 14, 3:00 A.M. THE CONFEDERATE ARMY CROSSED THE POTOMAC ON A MAKESHIFT PONTOON BRIDGE.

THEY RETURNED TO VIRGINIA, HAVING LOST AT GETTYSBURG, BUT READY TO FIGHT AGAIN.

THE END

The fighting on Northern soil in Gettysburg was the second time that the Confederate army had tried to bring the conflict into the North. The Maryland Campaign, which ended in September 1862 with the Union victory at the Battle of Antietam, was the first.

As they did after Antietam, the Confederate army retreated home, following the defeat at Gettysburg.

Gettysburg proved to be a critical turning point in the War Between the States. The Army of the Potomac had won an important victory under its new commander, General Meade. Meade proved to be a great leader, who listened to his officers and often took their suggestions. At Gettysburg, he wisely recognized the strength of the fresh Confederate cavalry and chose not to counterattack after Pickett's charge.

General Lee had asked too much of his army, while knowing too little about what was going on around him. Yet he was extremely fortunate to have escaped with his army across the

★ *The Union capture of Vicksburg, Mississippi, cut the Confederacy in half and opened the entire Mississippi River to Union gunboats and supplies.*

✯ (Above) *President Lincoln gave his famous Gettysburg Address on November 19, 1863.*
(Left) *Gettysburg was one of the bloodiest battles in American history.*

Potomac. If the Union forces had attacked the retreating Confederate army in force, the war might have been over.

Meade preferred to preserve his tired troops, rather than drive them on. He had met his objectives at Gettysburg: He had turned back Lee's army and driven them out of the North. However, President Lincoln was very disappointed that his army had won the battle, but failed to end the war at the Battle of Gettysburg.

While the fighting at Gettysburg was going on, the Union army took control of Vicksburg, Mississippi. This allowed the North to control the Mississippi River, the main transport route for each army's supplies and troops. The double victories at Gettysburg and Vicksburg boosted the Union army's morale, and they now fought with renewed energy.

The support that the Confederacy had hoped to win from Great Britain and France never came. The South now realized that they were fighting this war alone.

On November 19, 1863, President Lincoln gave a speech in Gettysburg, known as the Gettysburg Address. In it, Lincoln honored those who fought at Gettysburg and carefully explained the values for which the war was being fought. It is remembered as one of the most important speeches in American history.

# ★Glossary★

**artillery** Large, heavy guns that are mounted on wheels or tracks.

**breastworks** Temporary fortifications.

**carbine** A short-barreled lightweight gun originally used by the cavalry.

**cavalry** The branch of an army that was trained to fight on horses; cavalries use armored vehicles today.

**converge** To come together.

**decimate** To destroy a large part of something.

**deploy** To place in battle formation.

**dispatch** A written message.

**division** A large military unit that is smaller than a corps.

**draft** The selection of people for military duty.

**engage** To take part or involve oneself.

**flank** The far left or right side of a body of soldiers.

**forager** Someone who hunts for food.

**infantry** The branch of an army trained to fight on foot.

**infiltrate** To pass through gaps in the enemy's line.

**militia** A group of citizens who receive military training but who are on call only for emergencies.

**musket** A gun with a long barrel used before the invention of rifles.

**picket** A soldier positioned to protect his main army from surprise attack.

**rampage** Reckless or violent action.

**regiment** A unit of troops made up of two or more battalions.

**salient** Something that projects outward or upward.

**secede** To formally withdraw from a group or organization, often to form another organization.

**skirmisher** A soldier who engages in a minor fight with a small force of enemy soldiers.

# ★ For More Information ★

## ORGANIZATIONS

**The Gettysburg National Battlefield Museum Foundation**
P.O. Box 4224
Gettysburg, PA 17325-4224
(866) 889-1243
Web site: http://www.gettysburgfoundation.org/

**Gettysburg National Military Park**
97 Taneytown Road
Gettysburg, PA 17325
(717) 334-1124
Web site: http://www.nps.gov/gett/

## FOR FURTHER READING

Gaines, Ann. *Battle of Gettysburg in American History*. Berkeley Heights, NJ: Enslow Publishers, Inc., 2001.

January, Brendan. *Gettysburg*. New York: Da Capo Press, 2004.

Murphy, Jim. *Long Road to Gettysburg*. Boston: Houghton Mifflin Company, 2000.

Smith, Carl. *Gettysburg 1863: High Tide of the Confederacy*. Oxford, England: Osprey Publishing, 1998.

# ☆ Index ☆

## WEB SITES

Due to the changing nature of Internet links, the Rosen Publishing Group, Inc., has developed an online list of Web sites related to the subject of this book. This site is updated regularly. Please use this link to access the list:

http://www.rosenlinks.com/gbcw/gettys